First Facts™

Why in the World?

# Why Do Bears Sleep All Winter?

## A Book about Hibernation

by Mary Englar

**Consultant:**
Dr. Bernd Heinrich
Biology Department
University of Vermont

Capstone press®
Mankato, Minnesota

First Facts is published by Capstone Press,
151 Good Counsel Drive, P.O. Box 669, Mankato, Minnesota 56002.
www.capstonepress.com

*Library of Congress Cataloging-in-Publication Data*
Englar, Mary.
    Why do bears sleep all winter? : a book about hibernation / Mary Englar.
    p. cm.—(First facts. Why in the world?)
    Summary: "A brief explanation of hibernation, including what hibernation is, why animals
hibernate, and how they do it"—Provided by publisher.
    Includes bibliographical references and index.
    ISBN-13: 978-0-7368-6379-7 (hardcover)
    ISBN-10: 0-7368-6379-6 (hardcover)
    1. Bears—Hibernation—Juvenile literature. I. Title. II. Series.
QL737.C27E54 2007
599.74'44604543—dc22                                            2005037719

**Editorial Credits**
Jennifer Besel, editor; Juliette Peters, designer; Wanda Winch, photo researcher; Scott Thoms,
    photo editor

**Photo Credits**
Ardea/Francois Gohier, 15; Getty Images Inc/Image Bank/Bob Elsdale, 6–7; Getty Images
Inc./Taxi/Gary Randall, 18; Kevin Schafer Photography, 17; Lynn Rogers, 12; McDonald Wildlife
Photography/Joe McDonald, 14; Minden Pictures/Frans Lanting, 9; Minden Pictures/Jim
Brandenburg, 11; Minden Pictures/Konrad Wothe, cover (top); Minden Pictures/Mark Raycroft,
8; NASA/Johnson Space Center Collection, 21; Shutterstock/Howard Sandler, 5; Shutterstock
Kropotov Andrey, 10; SuperStock/age fotostock, cover (bottom); Unicorn Stock Photos/John
Ebeling, 4; Visuals Unlimited/Charles George, 16; Visuals Unlimited/Gustav Verderber, 20

# TABLE OF CONTENTS

# What Are These Animals Doing?

Deep inside a snug cave, a black bear builds a bed of dry leaves. Groundhogs and snakes slip into their underground **burrows**.

What are these animals doing? They are getting ready to hibernate. They will sleep through the cold days of winter.

# Scientific Inquiry

Asking questions and making observations like the ones in this book are how scientists begin their research. They follow a process known as scientific inquiry.

### Ask a Question

You rarely see geese in winter. You wonder, do they hibernate?

### Investigate

Begin looking for geese in the fall. Use a calendar to record how many geese you see each day. Use binoculars to watch for birds in trees and in the sky. Finally, read this book to learn why some animals hibernate through winter.

### Explain

You see fewer geese in winter, but you still see some. You also noticed flocks of geese flying south. You decide that geese migrate, not hibernate. Record your findings in a notebook—and keep asking questions!

# Why Do Some Animals Sleep All Winter?

When food and water become hard to find, some animals hibernate. During this time of rest, animals' heartbeats slow way down. Their body temperatures drop. These animals may not wake up to eat or drink for months.

**? DiD YOU KNOW?**
During hibernation, a hazel dormouse's body temperature will drop at least 50 degrees below its normal temperature.

7

Some animals, such as bears and raccoons, hibernate lightly in winter. Sometimes, they wake up and leave their warm beds to search for a little food.

A few animals hibernate during very hot, dry weather. This is called **estivation**. Desert toads dig down into the ground and nap until it rains.

# Why Don't All Animals Hibernate?

Some animals are able to find enough food during winter. Some squirrels eat seeds they buried in the ground. Wolves hunt animals in their **habitat**.

Most birds and insects **migrate** to warmer climates to find food. They come back from their long trips when the weather warms up.

# How Do Animals Know When to Hibernate?

In summer, there are plenty of grasses, seeds, and berries to eat. But as the seasons start to change, animals **sense** it's almost time to hibernate. They eat and eat and eat! They build up fat so their bodies will have energy during their long rest. When the days get shorter and food runs low, they hibernate.

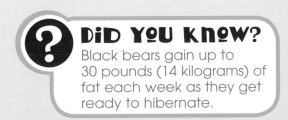

**? DiD YOU KNOW?**
Black bears gain up to 30 pounds (14 kilograms) of fat each week as they get ready to hibernate.

## Where Do Animals Hibernate?

Some animals, like bats, huddle together in old buildings or caves. **Dens** are good winter homes too. In their dens, animals are protected from **predators** and from the cold.

Some snakes in cold climates knot together in unused burrows or tree stumps. By coiling around each other, the snakes keep from freezing.

## How Long Do Animals Hibernate?

Animals usually hibernate through the coldest times of the year. Arctic ground squirrels hibernate for up to nine months.

16

Some animals may hibernate for a few weeks. Sometimes on a cold night, frogs may go into a light hibernation. They hibernate for only a few hours.

# How Do Animals Know When to Wake Up?

When the days grow longer and warmer, animals sense it is time to wake up. Light sleepers wake often and look outside. Other hibernators take several days to wake up. But for all hibernators, it's time to eat!

## ? DID YOU KNOW?

Every year on February 2, Americans celebrate Groundhog Day. According to legend, the groundhog peeks out of its hibernation home. If the groundhog sees its shadow, there will be six more weeks of winter.

Wood frogs live in some of the coldest places on earth. These frogs hibernate under leaves. But sometimes, temperatures fall so low that their bodies freeze solid! To survive, wood frogs build up a special sugar in their bodies that keeps their insides from freezing.

20

!

# WHAT DO YOU THINK?

Scientists study why and how animals hibernate. They think one day this information could help astronauts go on longer space trips. Hibernating astronauts would need less food and water. Best of all, they would not get bored on long trips. What are some other ways people could use hibernation?

# GLOSSARY

**burrow** (BUR-oh)—a tunnel or hole in the ground made or used by an animal

**den** (DEN)—a place where a wild animal lives

**estivate** (ES-tuh-vate)—to spend time in a deep sleep during dry or hot periods

**habitat** (HAB-uh-tat)—the place and natural conditions in which plants and animals live

**migrate** (MYE-grate)— to move from one place to another when seasons change or when food is scarce

**predator** (PRED-uh-tur)—an animal that hunts other animals for food

**sense** (SENSS)—to feel or be aware of something

# READ MORE

**Ganeri, Anita.** *Hibernation.* Nature's Patterns. Chicago: Heinemann, 2005.

**Murphy, Patricia J.** *Why Do Some Animals Hibernate?* The Library of Why? New York: PowerKids Press, 2004.

**Scrace, Carolyn.** *Hibernation.* Cycles of Life. New York: Franklin Watts, 2002.

# INTERNET SITES

FactHound offers a safe, fun way to find Internet sites related to this book. All of the sites on FactHound have been researched by our staff.

Here's how:

1. Visit *www.facthound.com*

2. Choose your grade level.

3. Type in this book ID **0736863796** for age-appropriate sites. You may also browse subjects by clicking on letters, or by clicking on pictures and words.

4. Click on the **Fetch It** button.

**FactHound will fetch the best sites for you!**

# INDEX